The Ruined Room

Also by T M Collins

Poetry

My Poetry
The Poetic Totem
Yabby Creek
Along the Lip's Edge
House of Voices
The Crooked Floor
The Cold Stones of Feeling

Fiction
Until a Shrimp Learns to Whistle

T M Collins

The Ruined Room

For Elizabeth,
and in memory of my uncle, Evan Collins, 1933–98

The Ruined Room
ISBN 978 1 76109 435 4
Copyright © text T M Collins 2000
Cover image: Nothing Ahead from Pexels

First published 2000 by Plateau Press

This edition published 2022 by
GINNINDERRA PRESS
PO Box 3461 Port Adelaide 5015
www.ginninderrapress.com.au

Contents

The Ruined Room	9
Painting Time	10
Changing Night	11
The Photographer	14
Never Any Sunlight	16
Standing Outside the Emergency Entrance	17
Windmill in the West	18
Bones of Contention	19
War	20
Anchor Wharf Theatre	21
To the Park Bench	22
Stepping on Motion (in the early morning)	23
Verticals at Night	24
Crow	25
Lonely Solitude	26
Escape (from Boggo Road)	29
Dropping off the Christmas Cake at the Priory	30
Coral Cay Diving	31
Disperse, 1877	32
One-arm Memories	33
Yelping	34
Lizard Across the Dotted Line	37
The Boy and the Bird	38
The Bonfire – A Family Funeral	41
Listen to the Ink	42
Memories in Glass Cases	43
A Candle Lit Every Year	44
At Ninety-one	45
As a Poet Reads	46
That Hat (red & green)	47

Australian Images – A Series of Poems	48
Canoeing	58
Ashes on Water – Suddenly Tossed	59
The Campfire	60
Communion	61
Farewell	62
Tantalise	72
Derelict, George Street	73
Abortion	74
His Dad's Shroud	75
Shivers of War	76
The Priest and the Farmer	77
Lost Souls	80
Things Remain	81
Suburbia	82
Spirit's Hill	84
Reading	85
Writing Ahead of Myself	86
Night Sky	87
I Think of You	88
Acknowledgements	89

Unfathomable Sea, whose waves are years;
Ocean of Time, whose waters of deep woe
Are brackish with the salt of human tears!
                              Shelley, 'Time'

The Ruined Room

A jute bag in the corner, university books
accommodate loneliness on the dusty desk.

There's heat in this room like a cage hoarded
with snakes, the window shut since last summer.

Dust in sentimental pose smears everything as
plenty of sunlight blasts into the room,

the curtains blush from the tangle of heat near
the windows, heat that is amplified by the ever-

present glass, this room is like a cockpit and
the design on the curtains is young aviators

having a go at the edge of adventure, the story
naturally ends there at the point of the seam,

at the stitched edge of these curtains, these
curtains are the only thing of prominence,

of colour, of life, that is left, left like
munitions after the battle is lost.

Painting Time

Subtitled: The Scene Painting Anticipation Until Another Day
for Amanda Townsend

The Scene:

Rushing grass, the wind pushing it down the slope. An inverted steel grey sky echoes upwards from the lake. At horizon's waist rainfall witters, moulded strokes of ash, the blotches of storm clouds sit snug into the corners of panorama.

Painting:

On the canvas the oil weeps, little blobs of artistic feeling. The backing board is touched by the paint's life fluids, the oil stain seeping through plywood. The power of art. The paint is securing itself, setting its roots.

Anticipation:

The ice of colour, the oil of smell, the ring of the canvas in the open air as if the canvas is singing to a frame, a hundred or so miles away, on some wall in a shop, that frame climbs and crawls about on a hook, waiting to close the scene.

Until Another Day:

Two paces back from the easel and the clouds are heavy industrial steel, the wittering rain now metal studs falling from a black sky. The weather, not the frame, closes the scene. As the car shoots lines of yellow light like cataracts along the soaking road the painting time will have to wait.

Changing Night

'The night will never stay, / The night will still go by, / Though with a million stars / You pin it to the sky; / Though you bind it with blowing wind / And buckle it with the moon, / The night will slip away / Like sorrow or a tune.'
– Eleanor Farjeon, 'The Night Will Never Stay'

Pewter sky, the gesturing night air and soon the slow slap and rub of rain. The yellow-backed bark of a dog caught on the end of a far from friendly leather-bound bone boot echoes under the canopy of evening, the night begins with the choking of faint sunlight, the tide of light drowning in the black sand and the gunfire of stars warn of much different sights, rain foaming in cloud's bellies dries to a signature of moisture. Softly convoys of darkness move in

surrounding the scene and the sway of the breeze, Tahitian girls revisited. Nights' breeze whinnies in the soot of the sky. The moon clubbed upwards to its perch, a half burrow dug into the black tree trunk of night. An aircraft all naked silver plucks at the shallow clouds, manoeuvres itself around the corner of night reaching a new morning at first stop. With the misty clouds and the stars a ghostly sketch is formed and buried in the depth of night, faint

inscriptions that can't be read. The distant hills shingle away, warped trees trellis the horizon as the gears of summer engage. The stars sizzle in the postcard distance. The perimeters of the scene, the panorama have polished staves holding up the sky, it is here where all poetry begins. Calliope bathing in the flakes of water matted into a tapestry of sheets in the crashing darkness. The wind yammers at the stars' thirsty eyes. But it is when the muse is asleep

on the beach that the eyes of the wind ensnare the water's surface like the tussling of hair. Eyes that drink from the reflected light. Happy eyes, grinning eyes resting atop those distant hills as the rain runs freely at their slopes like slaver. Clouds as lively as smoke blurted from chimney stacks mat the sky and the staves tighten, sideways thumbscrews. With Calliope still asleep the moon sneaks from behind the stage curtain, her body bloated in costume, she hangs from the rafters, resembling a bleached sack of oats and then as the muse awakens the tracery of the scene is etched into my thoughts. A small bonfire on the beach below beckons vision, the small brown bones of fire, a skeletal mass of flame, wounds of red embers, flames that snigger and grin. A gallery of white smoke sauntering upwards in drunken litanies, masking the

black air, disguising evening and those small brown bones twitch and snap in pain. A gentle shrug from the skeletal body, the whole mass moving under the weight of heat and airs' eyes weep, the sand slowly bakes dry as the tender-below is warmed like blood. In six hours the sky will no longer be littered with fragments of glass, and below a ring of singe will guard the fire-site, a pile of grey, black and white crumpled bones, those same small

brown bones, just gathered beach twigs. Off to my left the stout and blurred lights, the grubby glow of Surfers Paradise echoes with the trumpets of nightfall as vipers of dew settle, this place sits below a cocaine night, a night drunk and slunk unaware into days' nuisance clock, the arms of its existence as artificial as the light, the whipcords of glow choking blackless air. The night sky, here only is like black ice, the moon has maundered up, its skin

punished like white rhinoceros hide. This, the city of bilge-water thoughts. It is scalpel cold here, chilled like mildewed gravestone in winter glint and crisp of moonlight. Here, in the scuffle of the night the moon is a close-up of stained rotting teeth, it watches the wounded taxis queuing for food, craving the crinkled and chunky money as the scraps of clouds wipe the sky. Yet back here on my park seat nature polishes her shoes readies herself and past midnight's blank page, her fingers of darkness lonely turn each sheet of silence as the words of stars scurry down deeper into night, while the stump of time wears away fractionally by ever-present eyes. Black snow with white footprints, little cut out shadows hiding behind their master crystal images. The last page crinkles over in defiance of time's weariness, the printed page asleep as the white glowing cover of morning stirs all into readiness. As my

part of this city meets the dawn, curtains will be drawn and blinds stretched, peeled back against their cylinder spines. The sunlight prancing, setting glows in the hair of fruity beach girls. The murky eyes of night almost closed, light stoops up beach banks, up streets, over buildings like voices trailing. Night gone. Day walks across the park in an old man's face.

A number of lines from this poem have been used to germinate other poems in this collection. It has been done much like striking a plant from a cutting.

The Photographer

for Graham S. Burstow

'A photograph is not only an image (as a painting is an image), an interpretation of the real; it is also a trace, something directly stencilled off the real, like a footprint or a death mask.' – Susan Sontag

What gives you the power
dear photographer to
capture a moment, freeze
something in time, record
it in 'art and language',

what gives you the right
when for the writer to
capture the same (if they
do at all) they must hack
bone from stone. Often I

roam magazines for needy
inspiration, patrol these books,
books of photographs,
and it is these cold as lead
to touch photographs in these

coffee table magazines that
give the writer reason to urge,
reason to write from the urge
and then it is much a case of
excising the wasted flesh,

the words that are too
heavyweight in meaning.
Not so the photographer –
'only the photographer
can hold the tide'.

Never Any Sunlight

In my parent's home, that chaste place of memories,
where the doors clatter open closed by themselves,
they speak of dusty times, talk about life over so

many years, and that dust is the only living organism
inhabiting the confines of this abode like troubadours
prancing, settling, only moving when disturbed. With
curtains drawn and blinds peeled back against their
cylinder spine, you'd think sunlight would gallop in

but the gypsies of family, reflections of familial
history, cerebral recordings of suburban existence,
join hands holding back the sunlight, holding back

that cleansing light. Mother often quietly commented
to Father, 'The sun, it never enters the house.' This
memory somehow wounds me with unhappiness, a lingering
wound like salt or alcohol to a gash of flesh. Perhaps
I should gather that dust, settle it in a large jar,

uncap it at leisure, letting those fleshy tales of so
many years percolate about, but still without that
cleansing power of sunlight.

Standing Outside the Emergency Entrance

Stars smiling in the scuffle of night, the moon
a close-up of stained rotting teeth and winter's
wind, whiskers of ice as the black pond of night

watches over the driveway, awaiting the arrival
of another casualty of papery existence, a body
pulped in a can of a car. Wounded taxis queue

for fares of food, craving the crinkled and
chunky money and as scraps of clouds wipe the
sky two street lights each side of the drive

resemble blotchy zeros on sticks, the ambulance
swims the driveway, a yellow tropical fish and
still they look on. On a good night those stars

can look like an upright lace net, not tonight
though, the siren fades leaving a hugh hugh hugh
sound, night's death tune, the laboured breath of

a young man. his face each minute harder into plaster,
his face matching the doctor's starched white gown and
almost, almost as white as those smiling stars.

Windmill in the West

Windmill in the west stuck in red clouds
thick with nasty grey tinges.
The sky loaded, the earth buckles
as birds trip through the air,
wanting a branch.
Houses sit as cardboard
cut-outs in the visiting dark.
The fading orange sky
licks the ground.
The mill silent.
The wind far away on a mercy dash
with the flying doctor.
Barns and fences
glow like burning logs.
Blackness creeping, the mill
stands like a spur.
Sky and horizon becoming
one hall of darkness.
Squeak, a huge wheel is in
motion, the wind is home.

Bones of Contention

Paintbrush, fine strokes, delicate
sweep, brushing aside a cover.
Veil of sand lifted to
reveal craggy features
of someone ancient.

Gazing out of sightless
eye sockets, looking
at our world – their world.
Their first view in
thousands of years.

A jigsaw puzzle
laid bare, fragment
with fragment, tiny pieces
added to unveil the past.
Trophies lying idle now discovered.

Bones, bones, relics.
Who owns what's lying in the sand?
Rest in peace while you can
dear remnants of antiquity
for whatever it is worth.

War

Banal battlements, mounds of dead.
Littered bodies, a field of flesh.
Futile carnage, glory in slaughter.
Guns echo, more blood is shed.

White crosses mark the ground,
victory disguised in uniform,
innocence hidden with the soldier,
and bright victory's tokens.*

* The Victoria Cross: a bronze medal (originally cast from Russian guns captured in the Crimean War), depicting a lion on a crown with the inscription 'For Valour' while the reverse side has the date for which the decoration is bestowed and the name, rank, and regiment of the recipient.

Anchor Wharf Theatre

Hills of sand pushed into troughs, the sky protruding from another,

and all about people work like ants, in orderly concern while the sun sticks out of small squat boxes, boxes all lined up in sequence and

numbered like family funeral plots. A burly actor, the director's

son, pleasantly wayward looking, grabs grenade-like a waxed paper cup, he's not acting, thirst, as a bird that for weeks helicoptered about

lies still atop the water dome, occasionally jolting from the sudden

upward bolt of a bubble, a fountain, strength in reverse, imploding. Elsewhere, trees like friezes, replicas mass-produced, touched up to

suit, are slotted into rectangle cartons and as a spare sun, cellophane

disc, sits on concrete, clouds kneel in at the wall, watching a fruity girl place water in a tea chest, a sheet at a time, sideways, then more

sky, neatly packed like faces in a crowd waiting for the next show.

To the Park Bench

With the murky eye of the river forever in his thoughts,
the light stoops up the bank like voices trailing.
Night, chilled like mildewed gravestone in the winter

glint and crisp of moonlight, the fields of water
wisp, wisp, wisp away on the current's conveyor belt,
forever moving, the silt Puritan in its behaviour,
no storm nor tempest riles the emotions of that silt.

Joylessly he wanders the bank, wine bottle nagging
in his hand, the stout and blurred lights of the city
echo with the trumpets of nightfall, the vipers of dew

at his shoes, shoes wearing themselves to sandals,
the kiln of his mouth, warm, hot with swig after swig
of alcohol, causing litanies of gait. A possum in a
tree scrabbles surly in its furry coat, while below

those cold branches he folds himself into the wind,
wizens his thoughts, clamps that bottle to his chest
and attempts the crossing of the park.

Stepping on Motion (in the early morning)*

A cobalt figure with cloudy whiskers pads the cobblestones,
cobbles of stone that are here as decoration and our figure
is here as a definition of 'purpose'. A cocaine night, slunk

unaware into days' nuisance clock, the arms of existence as
artificial as the light, whipcords of glow choke blackless air.
Sound, any sound is close woven, not in tatters like suburban

sounds; city noise is often a soft whirr, faint clicking of
times' limbs, inching their way to full fractions like thousands
of wooden clogs clip-clapping, the echo becoming a click, then

a tick off into the tock tock of sound like cog wheels working
the cat's breath, the breath from within the beast to without
the beast, expelled in vapour that is a fraction of time, much

like the length of time it takes to tear a sheet of paper (similar
sounds), it is that small measurement of time, the exact rumination
of time as the cat pad-pads stones, all the time stepping on motion.

* Au Bonne, Switzerland

Verticals at Night

Pewter sky, the gesturing night air, the slow slap and rub of rain. The yellow-backed bark of a dog caught on the end of a far from

friendly boot echoes across the canopy of evening, the night begins with the choking of faint sunlight, the tide of light drowning in the

black sand and the gunfire of stars warn of much different sights, rain foaming in cloud's bellies dries to a signature of moisture.

Softly, convoys of darkness move in surrounding the scene and the sway of the breeze, Tahitian girls revisited. The moon clubbed upwards

to its perch, a half burrow dug into the black tree trunk of night. An aircraft all naked silver plucks at the shallow clouds, manoeuvres

itself around the corner of night reaching a new morning at first stop. With the misty clouds and the stars a ghostly sketch is formed and

buried in the depth of night, a faint inscription, verticals at night.

Crow

It bites the air, eyes hastily slung into its head.

In flight its body a feathered
black hammock stretched and
glowing in watery sunlight,

as it turns, wings marshalling
the sky it reminds me of a single
sculler in the quaking blue water,

and lastly I remember its claws lather like teeth.

Lonely Solitude

for Cheryl

On the mountain, I'm lonely
and there is solitude.
Loneliness sits beside me and
solitude the other side.
Missing my home, my dog, is
loneliness – things familiar.
Solitude is being alone
and with it can come loneliness.
Here lie the joy and torturous
feelings of the place up there.
But as the mountain is
a source of power, solitude
is at its highest and most
rewarding degree concerned with
self sufficiency or lack of it.
A productive union, a compassion,
a communion with oneself.
That is difficult.
Sitting on mountain top and
I am offered rewards.
Beauty and tranquillity
and that peace, a complexity
of sound yet simplicity of noise.

My heart pounding.
My breath whispering.
In my mind my body has already
fluttered down to earth.
I am transcended from
reality into integrity of
conscience. I can think.
I am what I feel.
I scream out, shout out.
I move my feet slightly.
I am blinded, think of
honesty and measure my guilt.
It is rewarding up here.
I understand.
I love.
I hurt.
I am introspective.
There is virginity of grace.
I meet myself.
My mind is open without
a noticeable door.
It will not close up here.
I am stimulated beyond all degree.

There is stillness
as clouds balloon in,
and birds rifle and wheel off.
The trees, the rustle, chatter of
the wildflowers, the earth and its rocks.
I am now alone not in dreams
but with the fear of real life.
The purity, the finer variety
of thoughts and impulses, messages
creating a living feeling, are
the rewards that will carry
through my times when not
on the mountain top.
Going back to the 'sad fragility of
humanity' gave me reason to search
the rewards on the mountain.
The integrity of lonely solitude.

Inspired by my first trek to the top of Mt Kosciusko

Escape (from Boggo Road)

Night sky like black ice, the moon maunders up,
its skin punished like white rhinoceros hide,
the wind yammers at the stars' thirsty eyes.

Metallic blue caps patrol the hills' skull, the
porcine occupants sniffing out their prey, a
backyard, clothes all entangled on the clothesline.

Nights' breeze whinnies in the soot of the sky,
the river, restful, flakes of water matted in a
tapestry of sheets, watches the hills shingle away,

warped trees trellis the horizon as the gears of
winter engage and the unshod feet resemble mushy
barnacles, running on wet streets of a city that's

a mausoleum at night. Hell is people not places.
Stars sizzle and in the distance the chimney stack
blurts smoke, laundering of uniforms, all blue-grey.

Light whirlpools about, running spotlights, the
quicksands of light squelchy like mud and the
porpoise-bellied man alights his vehicle, his bald

spot tapestried by a navy blue cap – he's a satirist,
always jibbing, his trigger twitches – the prey found,
now convent dreams give way to bilge-water thoughts,

a bell boy shape cowering, innocence yells from the putty of
his face as authority's leather-bound bone
foot jerks forward, dispelling all thought of escape.

Dropping off the Christmas Cake at the Priory

A dusty dying place of hymns, omens and ants. And on the desk a Latin book borrowing sunlight from the window. A handkerchief, yellowy, sticky, browning in spots sits like a dirty miniature sack beside the book.

He walks in like the sudden coming of a season, lilac licking about his frame. A rod of brown paper rests across the wall, itself trying to figure out its purpose. Outside the new blades on the mower help the gardener

think of golden-beached holidays, girls of salt and sea, the ocean blue green in their eyes. Rained up leaves block the corner gutter. That's the spot where Sister Isabelle fell last year, did her hip like snapping brittle

sun-faded PVC. Looking at those leaves I can almost see her tongue between her teeth in the quarters of pain. Inside again and age argues with wood-grained patience. A ball of twine green circled on the top of a

chair post. In a silver bowl a fallen candle, fragile wax and matches piled like bones, black tipped like vintage mildew. Then the braided sunlight, flicked back and forth through the trees, spreads codes of light pastiches

on the carpet. A medal featuring an old pope hangs from a dresser door handle. Pope John and a book of poems on the crisp made bed. A fountain pen. And that hankie.

Coral Cay Diving*

Whispers of bubbles popping through
the skin of water to explode
into particles of nothing.

Fractions of life floating secretly
about, unaware of the world
beyond their aquatic spot in time.

Filigree castles without a
sense of design, testimony
to life as a sculpture.

Coral cay diving amongst the waves as
the world passes around and over, no
interest in the echo of life,
a small animal's skeleton.

* Capricorn-Bunker group of islands, Keppel Bay

Disperse, 1877

'A country that only recognised Aborigines in 1967 has something to think about.' – Christopher Barnett

Not like snails to rain
more like lemmings to water.
What a generation, any.

Men of the tribe spear
white mens' stock and into
memory's shutter goes the result.

Disperse, disperse, disperse,
was the polished euphemism
for wholesale slaughter.

Hunted like rabid dogs,
it becomes a dreary tale
humans being thinned to extinction.

Not like snails to rain
more like lemmings to water.
What a generation, any.

One-arm Memories

Trees stuck in grass hills, the blue sky flies between the waterfalls of green at the tips
of trees, the wind spins, the scene is plastic-looking as if manufactured, perhaps
a giant fibreglass sculpture velcroed onto the edges of the horizon as sunny
clouds gather in the market garden of the southern sky, and as dead
trunks, stumps resembling refugees, never walk, but wait in
the compound. The flies thread in and out of my vision,
my solitary hand patrols across my face, waving like
a rudder being tested, my eyes blowing bubbles of
delight, little fractions of stars before my eyes
and as the afternoon shadows bend in pain
he strolls ahead, I follow, he carries his
instrument, carries it one-handed now,
he stops beside the blackened refugee,
I see his tanned volcanic rock-like
arm swinging the axe, with each
thrut thrut sound hitting the
refugee, just for the feel of
it, to remember, I flinch
and watch the stump
of flesh wobble.

John Paterson lost his footing while axing a tree, the axe sheering out of the cut in
the tree and severing his left arm just above the elbow.

Yelping

Silken insides, never seen waxy interior.
Tingling and rotating no retreating, stuck.
I drive on, my fingers grip your neck.
Steering on, control at the wheel.
A yelp and again you are looking at me.
Your bulldozer eyes crush my thoughts.
I hesitate, enjoy the soft scenery
as I move about in my seat, getting into
a rhythm of the road, dark and wet.
You grin, it reminds me of the garden
gate, as I twist my upper torso to
make this corner, and there's a yelp.
I run down the window, you tense your hip.
feeling like thrashing it around the
next bend, I hold back, gliding on.
The road giving thrills now, it's harder
to move about without losing control.
I heighten my temperament and put the
pedal down and down, yelps and yelps.
We're powering, the road is a
pulsating mass and my blood is boiling.
A soft yelp, as we speed closer
to our destination, faster and faster.

Closing my eyes, lights out, stupidity,
but fun at this speed, it's dangerous.
I'm beginning to sweat, you wipe my brow.
We're gushing along a tortured tunnel
and there is another yelp and my palms
feel stiff and a shiver zips up my back.

We draw closer, the air smashing about us.
I close my eyes tight, open and see the
straight line ahead, safe and ready.
I caress the pedal to the bottom and
there is that elixir of power and
the prolonged yelping stirs me to
drive faster and we are flying.
I feel cushioned against anything.
Suddenly a moth flits into scope and
lifting both hands up I grab for it.
One hand back down, you are restless.
The wings move in unison, a yelp.
At arm's length I stretch and clap
the moth, a waxy feeling in my
silken purse hands, as I crush the
moth's body and wings in mid-air.
Yelping and yelping as a ball of
fluff sticks in my palms.
I buckle forward as we hit the edge
of something on the road, a tree
perhaps, torn flesh and mush,
little explosions of tissue as
my mind is in delight.
You finger my temple as we lie
in a pile of smashed remains.

        or

Suddenly a moth flits into scope.
I buckle forward and catch it and
slam it between my hands as I

lose control and veer off.
It shivers in my palms, torn flesh
and mush, an explosion of tissue.

It is wasted and you look at me in
delight and gently finger my temple
and wipe bodies' tears away.

Lizard Across the Dotted Line

The stretching tongue, the rippled lips drinking at the liquid sky,
the neck straining at the blue flow, aching in delight,
the eyes chained to the gossamer glare of the midday sun.

The singleness of the day.

The rushing bitumen burns the colour black into the landscape,
the lizard lies like the cross stroke of a 'T',
the white dash below, drawn from its belly on the parched road.

The singleness of the lizard.

The Boy and the Bird

What sight has the bird,* a lonely passenger in time's wake, flying at ridiculous heights like a lout helium balloon navigating by an invalid sense,

losing half its body weight in a flight that will take 160 days no less, perhaps more, and what thoughts ink in calendar days, rotating tumbler days, spinning

in a treadmill of movement. Numberless hours, an infinity of minutes crunching like old hollow grains of sand. The sky-world full of no exquisite

bodies but the scattered debris of misted wind and yet up here angels set the imagined corners blowing trumpets and still a young child no more than nine

years has devotion to the water, like the birds' gluttonous devotion, his training in the watery dew of his mother's eye, is for the Olympics. She sits,

at the far end of the pool watching the young boy, watching the bird of her hopes, the bird of her dreams, the bird of her sex union, the result of that

union with the man she once loved, watching that bird in the boy, watching that misted wind as clouds and yet the bird is in training for nothing; our

angels sit on concrete posts, four Olympians† immortalised in statuesque training with the nerve of the bird etched into their sculptured faces, ten years

back now, greeting swimmers at both entrances, on top of posts, two to a gate, their bronze grace in brassy abundance against all the white of the future.

There are corners in the pool though none in the air. The bird and the boy both at a feast, both at a feast devouring times dribble spots, each spot of

dribble a second more than beyond the fifth bell making a minute, that's how Old Father Time got his name, dribbling time away, wearing it into psyche

like hot bitumen in sand. What pardon can you give the bird, its curse that it
needs to fly, the boy carries blood as his pardon, his mother relentless in her

sober cladding of hope for her son. In amongst the pencil stream of bubbles,
the minute release, like the expiration of energy from the wing tips are the

thoughts of the boy but the globular retardation of thought of the bird, if
indeed it thinks at all, impulses unsightly and worn crouching in the head of

seasons, but the boy has put a handful of thoughts linked into training
everyday, not a handful of marbles, six marbles like the claws at air, but

thoughts as in holding and reholding continually a fistful of sand, balancing
in water-weighted digits, as children often do, sandy time drifting

groundward swept by adult platitudes, not fun. We have but a short stay at
the world's desks of individual life, a short time to stay, we grow quick to

decay, yet the bird laden from flight, weak from having shorn half its body
weight, has a haste that is the quicker brother of decay. Would the mother not

be the bird rather than the boy, or is she perhaps more the rumour between
both. What meets that bird at the end of a numberless day is haste, the flying

through the rising of sun and the anchoring of moon like a prayer half sung
on an evening day or is it like the boy closeted in a watery weep pool of

midsummer dreams, his mother's mortgage of hope strapped to his chest like
a life jacket, would his father have put him through the torture of this

caricature of a hope, a blind faith in something more than a medal. In that
watery weep of a pool in the midsummer inkwell of thoughts, the thoughts

that ink in well, the monotonous lengths, the hours, the flaps of wings, the
strokes at air, the arcs of arm flesh through the crystalline water, slow fast

motions, bird and boy resembling bunting on a yacht's skeletal frame, that
boy mimics the antics, mimics the antics of the bird, flying each year, laps

half the earth to reach a land no more amorous to its needs, and what task the
swimmer but to clutch the medal. Remember, the boy, the bird, will both die,

nothing lives forever and even daffodils as quick as birth is new life, growth
is new decay. What surgeon put the mind and heart of a bird in this, that

featherless shape and as hours, minutes, moments, the dribbles of time, the
bird to a nest somewhere, the boy to a podium perhaps or to crouch in the

shadow of his mother's vaunted whim. There is that difference, the bird flies
wedged between the sandwich of night and day the boy sleeps and only the

glint and crisp of moonlight caresses his dreams of glory. The grinding bones
in fluid locomotion, the bird blind in its journey, the flesh picked at by the

spectators lining the route, those spectators the tiny nitwits of time known as
fractions and the boy his ropes of thoughts bartering each other with each lap

and the time set in each day, a pearl of growth in that life of decay, no longer
a young boy cast in this poem, but a relentless dream sketched with definition

but haphazard regard into a bird in cage.

* The Arctic tern is a slender red-billed tern, *Sterna paradisaea*, up to 38
centimetres long and having a white plumage with grey wings and a black crown.
Terns often migrate long distances. The Arctic tern breeds in coastal regions from
northern Britain to the Arctic and migrates to Antarctic seas in winter.
† The Australian Mean Machine relay swimming team.

The Bonfire – A Family Funeral

for Christopher

There is a funeral in their minds.
The train nearby tearing at the tracks.
The dusty golden sun kicked into the sky.
The water of the lake sounding like music.
A mum, a dad and a miniature child
living a bad day, ever so, so, slowly.
In the hay bales of existence where
each strand of straw is a thought
the funeral in their minds is drying,
crackling, withering, igniting a name in
the crunching heat and the train leaves as
the solid silence of the lake listens
to their son's name burning in yellowing straw.
They've prepared for the death of their son,
a last holiday together, the Disneyland of
true integrity out in the outback, a kid
wanting to see 'the bush' as mum and dad
pack straw around the sides of the framed
photo of a child beside a gum tree and…

Listen to the Ink*

The perimeters of the scene, the panorama with polished staves holding up the sky, it is here where all poetry begins. Calliope bathing in

the waters in the crashing darkness. It is when the muse is asleep on the bank that the eyes of the wind ensnare the water's surface like the

tussling of hair. Eyes drink from the reflected light. Happy eyes, grinning eyes resting atop the hill as the rain runs freely at the

slope like slaver. Clouds as lively as smoke mat the sky and the staves tighten, sideways thumbscrews. With Calliope still asleep the

moon sneaks from behind the stage curtain, her body bloated in costume, she hangs from the rafters, resembling a bleached sack of oats and then

as the muse awakens the tracery of the scene is etched into my thoughts, to then be painted on to the page – listen to the ink.

* Pepperina Hill, Lake Moogerah

Memories in Glass Cases*

for Jane Collins

Solitary and cold is time. Locked in confinement,
memories packed away tightly in cases of fingered glass,
these memories'll break if you're not careful, if you
don't think them regularly. Well what else is there
to do when the flame of wars' candle burns somewhere else.

Open those cases and spill life onto the hard floor,
talk of those times, pass them on, don't leave them
in mausoleum melody, case to case, event to event,
tales told in the depths of night, you must speak
them often, then time will be chiselled with peace

and the horrific sheet of incarceration of these
memories torn up. Then no longer on a certain day
will old old men and women walk grey streets with the
week's prior newspaper headlines caressing memories
like the touching fingers on those glass cases.

* War Memorial, Canberra

A Candle Lit Every Year

for Bobby Sands

The flame absorbs my thoughts, my memories past, and memories to be drawn in the future flicker in moods of glowing impatience. Gazing at the centre of quivering, wavering, quavering it speaks back at me,

questioning my search for that which is beyond the individual, yearn for the knowledge, the nostalgia of memory, the inking into mind's castles of trophies that are worthy remembrances. This candle, images

living with resonances, accompanying it – the behaviour of the candle is the peace I yearn, although beautifully destructive, terribly conformist in style, the candle snickers, mirrors my thoughts, collects my memories

and translates them into words, paring them into lines with a soft eeriness and making those words resemble the black smoke floating freely away, not reined in by forgotten thoughts.

At precisely 1.17 a.m. on 5 May 1981, Bobby Sands died of starvation in Maze Prison after a 66-day fast.

At Ninety-one
for Mop Bradley

Climbed into his car,
with trembling hands,
let go the brake, ran

a finger over flattened
lines, towns on his
tattered touring map.

He did not drive out
of the garage as he'd
been everywhere before.

As a Poet Reads

For Robbie

You with your marble art look, idolatry inched sideways into your eyes, the flick of your hair heavy, laden with him. The cloth that covers your milky skin brown and black and boots that match, trace the hemline, the bulge and budge of your breasts as you sigh, a sigh like a cut fish, silver, wet and alone.

I watch you move, the pursing of your lips like a bleached prune, you never wear enough make-up. Angry and confused like packed windsocks ready for export are your hands (those hands so used to expressing your dark dark desires) so limp on your lap, the folds of black material, warm black on white

flesh. You watch him on stage, he the imagist, the images of images catapulting from his mouth, trapezing ahead of his forehead, slightly rigid, these little word figures grab at your attention, your senses tease on his every word, and he's yet to glance at you. The tremor that will be his glance begins

abseiling your legs, that black cloth, a skin to be peeled, feels warmer now on your flesh, heavier, noticeable, it grips you like his hug. As the audience claps miniature thunder claps, like hundreds of fish flipping in an aluminium boat, he sees you. And I leave.

That Hat (red & green)

for Leonie

Black trees
branches wayward

scratch etch
scariness on

the window
pane night.

That hat appears,
beneath – a figure

shuffles the path
Christmas drinks, it's

almost midnight yet
the young child

waits, his face
smitten on glass.

Australian Images – A Series of Poems

1. The Sea

Waves mown fresh by the wind,
blades of water curl to the sun
and drip to a bed of alfoil moisture.

2. Goods Yard

A railway siding, the smell of coal.
Rails of polished hot metal,
looking soft in the crinkling haze.
A lone figure walks the flat steps
of dirty gravel and rivered wood.

3. A Lost Trinket

A bent grey spoon lost in a
village of ordinary grass.
Some child's first birthday trophy.
An inscription blurred in the
distance from here to my feet.

4. Corner Paddock

Leaves twisting, arguing, moving,
hiding behind each other, then
showing twittering movements.
Cows horn the air with their heads,
a jerky yet gentle upward motion.
Occasionally they look back. At what?
The paddock blisters and a hawk
skates the blue ink.

5. Tidal Pool

A fish flips, flaps helplessly,
a pool dammed. A rusty red crab
jockeys from side to side, definite
movements much like jukebox
selecting a disc, pushing
the wind from its sand hole.

6. Hot Bread Shop

Helmets of heat flog up from
the furnaces as metal starfish
shake the air with dust and
that delightful aroma.
Coins bounce, and one twirls on
a pale pale green glass counter
as the flags of linoleum curl
on the floor which is spotted
by tiny seeds that wink
under your feet.

7. Combing Her Hair

In my oblong retriever a small
row of struts floats effortlessly
through a red mass. The row of
struts tortoiseshell in colour.
My palms impatient on the wheel,
I lose sight of her as the plastic
spokes in my hands pulse me forward.

8. Hotel

Grass plugs itself into the
red brick wall, blistered
towers of grass living on
moisture, the smell of
alcohol tricking the mortar
into thinking it is glue,
crumbling foundations.

9. A Road

A drink can guards the road
as sand whistles along
a hole in the wind.
A truck canoes the road,
a black belt buckling
in the haze as the smell of
matted hair edges air.
The can moves on the
parched carpet, it pirouettes
from the flog of air the truck
expels, with the last sound
being the wet sigh of
twenty-eight rubber feet.

10. Rail Bridge

The bridge chiselling each rock face
end to end like a stiffened tongue.
Disappearing into a tunnel a
lead lump crawls two tin threads.
Closer and a constant trop trop trop
sound spears the soot-charged air.

11. Fishing

A fish climbing a line to breakfast.
The angler in disbelief, twirling his
excitement in cold fingers.
The nylon thread glints in
sunlight, a rasp of shine and
the first blink of day.

12. Fern

Leathery feathered brilliance of
polished healthy green.
You trick tremble the wind to
brush you once again.
It's that wind that polishes
your fleshy architecture.

13. A Circus

From small wooden peg,
tapped neatly into soil,
ten-foot length of rope,
tethers a tree trunk size leg.

14. A Truck

A truck coughs, clears its throat,
ticking up through a shaving.
Lights on its forehead patrol the
bitumen, black tar joined at the
dotted line like a snake peeling.

15. Morning

Rain washes dust from the stars,
cleans the stained moon as the sun
inches up on an invisible thread of heat.
Dreaming trees come to life with a
whisper, wind powder sprays the
sky a blue kite of brilliance and the
hot wood of the earth sucks in the rays.

16. Beach Towel

Quapp, quapp, quapp, quapp.
Sand shoots at your torso.
Flag the towel clean,
fold it mid-air, slot it
under your arm.
Bag tapping knee, radio
scuffing thigh,
the sun is setting.

17. Office Work

The hour hand tongues
its way around the face
and as the sun slippery
slides through the window
pigeons scooter about outside.

18. The Moon

A neat circle
made by a
one-hole punch.

19. Cycling

The spokes speak
a special dialect
like racing clocks.

20. Funeral

Walking outside a green
wrought iron fence I see
a child walk towards the
rusting gate, his tears
like gentle tin waves
fondling the water's
complexion of his face.

21. Storm

Clouds smoulder in the burnt
orange sky as in the distance
chains of lightning ladder
to the encrusted earth, each
link spasms in mid-air, birds
seek safe haven as a heat
haze filters upwards like a
venetian blind opening, the
sky heals to a darkened scar.

22. Clothes Hoist

Remains of a lead sculpture
genuflecting in the backyard.
Clothes wobbling like aspic and the
drops of water fall weighted, often.

23. Food

Stale feta cheese clouds
mould in the fibreglass
dish of the sky.

24. Country Hospital Veranda

The sun, the effective bandage
covers all. The sunshine like rain
simmers from the heavens.

25. Weather Change

Wind-flattened grass, running
down the slope, moving grass.
The sky navy vessel grey.

26. The Lake

The lake chops itself into
massive pools, glimmering like
oyster cults, flesh floating.

27. Night Theatre

Clouds smoke in the night sky.
The moon sneaks from behind
the stage curtain, her body
bloated in costume, she hangs
from the rafters, resembling
a bleached sack of oats,
it is the monologue part.

28. Dawn

Carbon fibre morning, the wink of the dew,
the collapsing of the black-starred blanket
backwards into the rotisserie of morning.

29. Dusk

The marble blue, flecked
with flame-light shudders,
the day bellows and hunches
over in prayer to darkness.

30. Campfire

Light the cannibal of darkness
swallowing particles of night.
Day long since dusted into the
hallowed galleries of landscape.

31. Petrol Station

Across a sea of liquorice
mechanical molluscs slink.
They feed from nutrient
rich tanks of fluid.
Robotic arms stuck in
the sides of their shells.
Amidst carpets of grease, grime
and dust, other molluscs sit.
insides exposed, awaiting recovery as
another is hoisted to fibro clouds.

32. Raining

A priest saying mass,
the window runs with stars,
the wind in training, darkness
escalating, time lolling about as
the droplets fall with feet of clay.

To be continued…

Canoeing

Like bone teeth gleaming in the water,
surfacing for food, patrolling the lake.

The water thick, thick as the fur at a dog's throat.
Ducks peck the surface like pigeons pecking

the iron coloured pavements in the city.
But this is the country.

As the trees kneel in at the wind like monks
at the altar, still the teeth patrol off,

looking for food, leisure.

Ashes on Water – Suddenly Tossed

for Trevor Moy

Wrought-iron wind creases sails as you patrol the deck and watching
from the bank is the upright lace lizard, then in cutting flashes of
sunlight the glow shifts in conversation and the lizard is lace white
like a brackish figure alone on shore. Winter's wind cuts throats as
the frosty sun poses that dilemma of colour, combinations of colours,

thoughts and your eyes glint green as the boat rows itself out on the
will of the current, the sea dark green, dark blue, silver, even white,
always changing colours. Sunlight is funny in conversation. Light and
colour talking, rapidly. The flash of the hull, a glint to shore like
Morse code or a single cat's claw hitting out. Layers of thought match

the matting of water, overlapping in a tumbling motion, the sloshing
mind of the sea, recurring children's dreams. Then the boats, bastards
of timber, plastic, materials like dreams, those hulls like children
lined up in life's dormitory. Things, all sculptured into the water,
all dressed in pyjamas of colour and as you stroll the deck the light

constantly talks at you. Time is idle, it is etched into peace in the
sea's existence. Then. From the ashes suddenly tossed on water the
lizard paints a picture, over and over again, the tumbling thoughts of
the sea and always that film of ash on water as the lizard stands alone
on shore, left to roam the perimeters of thoughts, forever, forever.

The Campfire*

Small brown bones of fire, a skeletal mass of flame,
wounds of red embers, flames that snigger and grin.

A gallery of white smoke sauntering upwards in drunken litanies,
masking the black air, disguising evening and those small brown bones

twitch and snap in pain. A gentle shrug from the skeletal body,
the whole mass moving under the weight of heat and airs' eyes weep,

the soil slowly bakes dry as the tender-below is warmed like blood.
Six hours. The sky no longer littered with fragments of glass,

a ring of singe guards the fire-site, a pile of grey, black and white
crumpled bones, those same small brown bones, only gathered twigs.

* Charlottes Pass, summer 1987

Communion

Crimson tongue glittering on granite thighs, beads of sweat like
cottages across a barren plateau devolving colonisation of emotion,
passion and love to intimate vibrations like a tapping chisel on

marble. Flesh milky grey in day's murdered afternoon glow as hearth
of hair, branching twisted, upwards in delight, the pyramid black on
bleached sand, anchored in delight like a tree sewn in earth's glory,

a knuckled strolling finger flicking at internal physical thoughts,
the half notes of desire, the pre-triggerings of climax, the gentle
splicing of flesh, morning's rose opening with the crystal weight of

dew, in the rumination of desire the act enters its intricate phase,
a haze of flesh ghosting into the dimming light, nibbling at the room's
personage, the hum of breathing strolling the confines of the room like

hovering doves in a flight dance of peace. As the rushing blackness
inks in, heads join, necks ache and pure pearl diamonds are shed,
broken shards of love, tears, stars sighing in reply at love's union.

Farewell

for Gwen Harwood

'Death is but a last farewell to all the difficulties, pains, and hazards of life.'
– (A modern interpretation of) 'The Swan and the Stork', Aesop's Fables

'I hope your images don't come back to haunt me when I'm in the geriatric ward.' – Gwen Harwood (from correspondence relating to this poem, 1992)

In here, death comes
as often as falling leaves.
I came here for peace,
to die eloquent and happy,
but instead when I blink
thoughts bleed and any
hopes of freedom shrivel in
hidden corners of this cold room.
Muddy blood in my veins
and my fingers bent with
an ageing distress.
I'm like a shaved fowl
roaming in yard of feathers,
hoping to be transformed.
Scorch marks, all named 'Reality'
walk the corridors of this place
singeing the walls with diatribe –
'He had a good life.'
'She lived life.'
'He's old now, but it doesn't matter.'
'My she had a full life, and now
it's her turn to move on.'
New faces appear like clouds
and disappear just as quickly.

The armies of worries and the
hurting gaze of tension walk
slowly across my shoulders and
occasionally tap my neck in defiance
of my riffling thoughts, and,
a tablet is dissolving in a
glass of water beside my bed.
The shadows in my throat,
images drifted from my head,
singers' voices building in
strength until they choke my
windpipe. The pain screaming
at me, suspicious of my requests
for quiet. But then – his voice.
The combustion of his voice stops,
shaking the wall into stiffness.
Time is like a crippled slug,
so slow, I think to myself.
I trowel my forehead of the
ornamental veil of fever and
my father's words, as he began dying,
come spear like, jabbing into my head.
'When the time comes son,
settle up the tally,

stack the cubes, make things tidy.'
And the chaplain just
yesterday or was it today?
'Death is a sugar tomb, sweet and final.'
Yet all I vision is a kettle
boiling dry and the gradual
quietening of its exhaling breath,
and a final faint crack of
hot metal. Then there is a
cantilever bridge swaying
from bank to bank. Ridiculous
thoughts, playthings lying in
mind's little kindergarten.
Or is it some crawling insect
of my psyche leaving a
last trail of bedevilment for
my conscience to bury,
the thread worm willowing
its way through a blister
in time to return as a
hauntingly gentle smile
on a young girl's face.
Days go and I strain
the room for a glimpse
of sight, a worthy reward
for open eyes, but my vision
is slain by that flexible
impulse, pain. Blind, my eyes
victims, and my body a cave
obliged to welcome more guests,

members of the cult group
called Illness. Again I listen.
Monotonously I listen, for his
constant breathing. It is so
relaxing. Only yesterday a
young boy visited me. I knew
nothing about him. He seemed
distressed. patted his hand
and comforted him. Then I rode,
turned the corner and there he was,
one hand clenched, the other open,
fingers wavering like sea fronds
beckoning wayward fish. Indeed time
is like a crippled slug, so slow.
The silver path that is left,
the entrails of history.
And that path links here
to there. The slug on the edge
of time erases on. I listen.
Listen. I half watch.
Finding the spot marked X
was not hard, it was on the
waxed map. My mind revels
yet sometimes stops dead
in its tracks, like the life
of a native tree deprived
by ground choked with
foreign seed. It's nearly
Christmas by most road signs,
but the mistletoe hangs dead.

Suddenly his voice thumps
the glass pane. He is singing
a tune to me. I listen as
my arms get whipped by what
feel like pine needles,
a gesture of hope,
my bones sit idle,
rusting pipes in soggy banks,
my muscles a shrinking marsh
and my body suffocating
under its own weight.
Tiredness is closing
like a nut on a bolt.
I must stay awake.
My friend outside is
chattering away colouring
the room with rich humour.
Another thought hammers
through the grey plasticine
reporter as a warm dripping
sensation echoes and then
slowly inches into dangling
shards of pain, wriggling
through my tissues.
The painful dart of old age,
and its treacherous spiral staircase.
I swallow the ache of a breath
and finger my pity,
then flick it aside.
My heart is a torn windsock,

billowing about in the
relentless wind. Suddenly
my friend's diminuendo
ceases and the wall
again cowers into silence.
His is an easy existence,
the regularity, the purpose,
whereas I'm like some
distant unattended life
support system clicking
towards the designated hour.
My lips, brittle leaves chilled
in snow, tremble as my mind
casts back, the line of time
tightening to reveal the
four leaf clover plucked
from the lawn as my young
brother playfully ate grass.
I questioned all things then,
except death, and now it
questions me. Lying in long
shadows my limbs are in painful
tranquillity, no exertion.
Quietness unfolding, the soul's
realtor must be awaiting a sale.
The walls are sullen,
the air is dripping with despair,
the ceiling seems low, moving closer,
a falling layer of paint.
Where is he? Where is my companion?

My company? Listening is painful.
Soon the chaplain will kneel
and pray for my inner being to be
lifted above the horizon and
escape to the land past dreaming.
But what of my body? My body
full of humidity and my half
eaten face will show stained
reminders of humility and
plastered on my chest still
those burn marks. Now I hear
my friend nattering to me or
perhaps to the pigeons, who,
I imagine, have become his
closest companions. What is happening?
My mind needled with pain
as the corners of the room
shift uncomfortably. A silver
hood will soon drift down and
cover my human features.
I see all manner of things,
trays of food and
black ribbons on the bed.
And that flimsy cardboard
sign 'Refused Transfusions'
on the bed head. This is all
a dream, I'm not dying,
it is just my mind's trigger.
There isn't really a sign above
me meaning to belie my true beliefs.

Again a gate is swinging and the
zip is nearly up on a clown's gown.
I see a leaf stop cartwheeling
across a sculptured lawn.
White smoke is being set free,
they have chosen a a new
fraternal leader. The dust
settles on a stiffened cloth
over a polished table as the
meeting begins. This meeting
will change the face of our world.
Across the room my little mate
is chattering away, talking ever
so calmly, I feel occasioned
to jump up and applaud his generosity.
But there is the burning bush
and a desert with a distant bell tolling.
The wind is thunder
and my name is being etched
in the sand by thousands of ants,
no doubt they tracked the
sniggering knell over the sands.
I'm being marshalled off
as the chaplain genuflects
and wipes his hands on his
brown gabardine robes.
Clenching my eyelids
in a cramp I see a crypt
with flames in it.
There is a cube of water

and a maze of corn
and a candle burning
in solemn delight,
each flicker a note
of joyful praise,
a simple song buffeting
the walls and evoking
sentimental images.
My friend seems
long departed. No pigeons.
I'm alone. I am, that
wretched fowl, I think,
as my mind feels tiredness,
it crouches, my thought's
hands supporting my mind's face.
The wick of the candle seems
to twist about in a sordid
display of self-torture as a
small sparrow somehow enters
the room and circles twice over me.
He looks grubby in brown-flecked
garments, not unlike the chaplain.
The wings are frayed and torn.
I notice this most.
Then I imagine a bubbling fountain.
This must be it, where is my friend,
won't he say goodbye? This torrid
encounter with life must be near finished.
I ponder how my body must
resemble an alabaster ornament.

I see children in the fields
of harvest, and a lantern swinging
without a light. My blood is nudging
along, not tossing, but sludging
like thick mud. I sight ashes in a
silver dish and hear cymbals clanging.
The young boy sits dressed in a
navy blue marching uniform beside me.
My thoughts pant for want of a
maniac's conversation. The talons
of memory dig deep as I see the
gaunt figure on the cross.
Lightning arcs across the room
making the air cringe and my final
moans soap the walls clean then
cloak them in a curse of geriatric despair.
The last sound I hear is the
air conditioner on the ledge outside.
He actually did say goodbye.

Tantalise

Son of Zeus, betrayer of
your father's secrets.
Condemned for this
cringing dishonesty.

Encased in water,
liquid air lipped and
mollified your foundations.
Above you a bulging branch
twitched, its delectable
fruit pulsing with ripeness.

Wanton your desire like
a kite lusting a breeze,
you snatched for food,
stooped for water.
Both drew away, the
water whirlpooled into Hell,
the fruit tugged up to Heaven.

Still you persisted,
still they receded.
Only your name remained,

Tantalus.

Derelict, George Street

Scabby and bleak his face, he humours himself, his stimuli,
the clouds, the footpath, even me.
He survives on faded memories, sitting beside a grotesquely
darkened building, one of society's

black bears, unwashed and roaming its ancient foundations.
The self-indulgent figure, he is
the central horror of his own dreams like the eye of the
cyclone, he's a lost folk hero,

hair steel wool, eyes alone, beard travelling, it's a sharp
image with a touch of fantasy,
yet he looks important amidst this environment, important
because he has not yet joined

the bears in stony silence. For me as I pass him his card
of lonely death is well hidden
in his looks, he explores me like explored clouds, no words
pass between us, mine are only

desperate attempts at breath, his is an orchestrated smile.

Abortion

for George and Maree

He stands courageously beside
his wife's prone body, waiting.
It is not polemic that they
(husband and wife) decide to
remove the disfigured foetus.
You cannot uglify the scene further.

He watches as the small figure
is plucked from her torn womb.
Holding the temporary bundle
of life, tears cut his flesh.
The small mass wriggles in his
hands and in the final throes
of death's dance he gently
closes his eyes and clutches the
tiny shell of life to his chest.

He wonders how his wife will feel
never having seen her son.

His Dad's Shroud

Like a linen map hung loosely from the wall, grubby and stained, the faded logo of a bread company, like some rare cloth, old and cracked, important. The grime is his facial grime. It hangs fastened to the lounge wall, a wooden batten (a strut from an old veranda deckchair) holding it straight. It hangs

as the last reminder of his dad. They wrapped his head and shoulders in that cloth moments after he died in the grain silo, a latch snipping open to let a cloud of grain pummel his workday thoughts, they wrapped his head and shoulders in that shroud, the grain dust like moth flesh on a hot light globe.

His colour, colourless like coral. life faded out, the stain of death imbued now in the fine fabric like tiny plankton in the sea's water skin. And that sinking feeling as they pulled his body from the shallow grain pit, the grain pulsing out like pebbled redless blood. The pale gaze of crows nearby, the

tip of his shoes still-black, the rest of the leather, brown, his eyes open, a fish's cold stare. The shroud hangs like an artefact. The kitschiness of it points at my thoughts. His crucifix, his cross, the lifetime of work on the farm, no recognition, but, my memory. As I patrol the room, thinking, my

thoughts thud-clanking like a door against a rusty gallon drum, I see, as I always see, the blotch of grease, grime packed into the shallow weave and cross of fibres. I trace my thoughts across each thread – the day he drowned in that grain silo.

Shivers of War

Thousands of shadows,
human shapes, figures numbered.
Everything walled by the luggage of wind,

pinned at all corners, invisible.
Journeying, the weather struggles at the landscape.
Planes arrive at midnight.

Lights along the runway create a delicate woven web.
Light buried into distant darkness.
The moon chafing at its black leash recording all the years

of unhappiness, worn into the leather collar of time.
From strictured beginnings the child bedevils existence
re-inheriting the placid fragile thoughts of landscape.

Like balcony rails the horizon protects the young child
from wandering, bequeathing safety. Then as twilight
sprinkles inward silhouettes, shadows leave from the

outer terraces of the scene. Those human shapes,
thousands of figures watching day shiver into night
as the child patrols the runway, waiting.

The Priest and the Farmer

They visit, return each year like migratory birds drawn on wisps of air, cajoled by longitudes and latitudes of wind. They sit in pews like dulled frames of those birds on branches. They are members of the local community joining together at Christmas, Easter, and occasionally if a death worthy. The most popular time is Christmas, as if a curse is unravelled upon those who don't show. A gesture like the forever ritual of hanging scant decorations, the garland at the front door like some ribald artefact. Out this way 'community' is a word thought to relate more to the city and its inhabitants. But it is the weary road travellers who creep their

vehicles onto the parched churchyard, probably seeing this religious place as an icon in the hills, an attraction after a morning's drive through the dusty dirty never-never of this most uninhabitable of countrysides. Yet the priest visits the dying, preaching to the uninterested, trying desperately to illuminate their lives. 'With God's Grace I Save Souls' written on his invisible business cards, invisible, for what use does this priest, what use does he have for business cards. In the church he stands an ordinary man elevated to pulpit status goading parishioners like sheep. He has a vintaged grin and facial bones refined, educated by forty years of

speaking. There is a spare beauty about his frame, youth in age and eyes stiff in determination never seeming to blink. The flocks of hair above each ear resemble two equal puffs of cloud hanging above a craggy cliff face. He speaks, endeavouring to chip away at the granite congregation. A mass of faces, blank satisfaction, a bare wall. It is the crying child in her father's arms that causes the stiff upper lip to bend further upwards, churning towards Heaven. A different child every week. Why do travellers take such young children with them? Why? Indignation. His eyes spit dissatisfaction at the distraction. All this painted into the lost memory of another Sunday morning as sunlight gauntly creeps across wooden floor to collapse at polished black shoes, shoes coated in a sheen of of dust, a protective wax. The farmer stands, pen in the inkwell of landscape, alone in field, in a paddock, his paddock, grasses like yellow and green bones buried upright in memory of thoughts of all country folk, this image is of course silly only in the sense that bones are dead, grass is not. Clods of crude earth sun themselves and at night moon's wind like a blunt blade slices blindly at landscape. Standing in that paddock is poetry, the disused tractor, rusting in its above-ground cemetery,

surrounded by blue air, it is coffin-bogged where it stopped, loosing its last breath, the heart of the beast expired with the thumping of a pedal, the human foot having such power. Yet it stands, like a poem dictated by the priest to the congregation of landscape, words working on into solid black hours of morning, every morning. Poetry, scribblings, in margins of the Bible, almost every page defaced, in blank account books, on any form of paper. Poetry in the vestibule each night, prose at the pulpit and science lying decaying in the corner of the paddock, sucking mud draining blood from the machine, draining it to a rusted heap. As the farmer

glances back over his shoulder, in a tumble-wheel of thoughts he casts back to the calender date of his birth, he realises that the opposite of poetry is science and that prose is the watering-down of thought, the collapsing of the card house, colourful. Anyway this is how he sees it. Religion is science, poetry his faith and prose what he has extolled to the congregation for forty years. Poetry is hunger, prose the feeding, and science the dieting, the being selective, farming the land. This is the doctrine of an ordinary man who clambered the land in his robes only to find solace in words, his words not from the weighty leather-bound book he was handed some forty-five years earlier. The farmer, next Sunday's priest, looks about his paddock, glances at the machine in the corner, its cold insides dead, just as the cold insides of the typewriter on the desk in the church are dying, almost dead. A final poem is waving in the distance of tomorrow's thoughts. The last poem from the priest, from the farmer. Sunday. The babble of the congregation, the hum of the landscape through open windows, windows that have never been shut. Then as if heralding an end to tranquillity forever, a utility chews the shoulder of the road throwing up hailstones of dirt and rocks. Beside the church boundary fence a road

traveller alights from the vehicle and begins urinating in the tall yellow grass. That road traveller is etched into the drifting shadows of the church. Nightfall is eating day. The priest stands with dusk on his shoulder listening to the babble of his imaginary congregation, the landscape murmuring. The traveller gone. Day gone. With the mass ended the priest retreats from the church. The farmer walks to the corner of the paddock. The shotgun like an appendage. Within a split second the hush of night is splattered with the dreams of an ordinary man. Science won out in the end. The following Sunday the church for the first time in forty years is packed.

Lost Souls

Lapping limestone cliffs, the water mumbles constantly
at the missing souls, the rescue boats long since painted
into seascapes that hang in dusty galleries, paintings
don't tell the facts – missing sailors stumbling around
in the cave of the sea, at first exploring their new home,
then with time they run about in blind panic, their eyes
shut forever, the stinging salt water dissolving flesh,
skeletal treasures, huge polyps in the grotto of the sea.
Wildly the silt is churned from the silky bottom, floating

upwards, dusting bones, limestone cliffs worn away, slowly.

Things Remain

for Madonna (and her mum)

With trepidation, like wandering about the house
across broken shards of glass, igniting memories,

stinging grief collected in long linked thoughts.
Death, the rusty razor blades of living, the ugly

superficial swipe, slashing at life's painting and
years later the angry eye of the camera relives

those lashings of memories, lashings tied loosely
on the sleeve page of a close family, children

remembering but glimpses when questioned, the
shavings of intellect most young, streaks of

memory, messages between parents and children.
One thing remains, a calendar date smeared with love.

Suburbia

Haunted by arthritic concrete orchardists, suburbs rise with distant powderings of noise, a mummified sound, suburbs like coffins, noise like

smells, but nothing else, no life, just houses of droll leaning through each day doing nothing off par, out of the ordinary, marooned in the bitter air of

the concrete, roofs fade into each other, bricks as if all borrowed from one massive fallen skyscraper built on mounds of clay, the clay denying true

earth as children's voices run up and down scales of happiness then are dented into a subdued state like milk bottles, just when or how many times

do you get the same bottle back? Sprinklers flaring water at the sun, the neighbourhood sounds are limp, the cars drugged in the streets and the

slow blowing of a drill, a power drill, as black birds as sinister as sand in the city lumber across the sky, a young boy looks up from his overturned

bike as if to say 'Why birds'? On a window latch hangs a white plastic bag, the remains of laughter drying from the trip to the swimming pool,

plastic has value in this household, not so four doors down, or is it up the street, the yard littered with shreds of silver paper, product creature of a

cigarette company that's been mown, intended to be cycloned up by the blades but only shredded across the lawn, silver thoughts of the mower

man scattered on his grass, soulfully. Letter boxes with the same label point out across the road at each other like rectangular cannons some

resembling boxed faces in an abstract sense with grotesque cylindrical bodies while at the corner grass drags itself like a wet sheet up a paling fence and the signpost for that street stands mysterious without its inverted rudder which now adorns a youth's bedroom wall eight blocks in another direction. Echoes

wait in this neighbourhood for the school bus to be replenished with the shrill vocabulary of schoolchildren. Almost winter and a cold crisp night to come,

the sky black and tethered to the moon's back and high in the sky are half supported stilts of cloud smoke and without a thread of breeze these columns

of smoke cloud build upwards. Another nightbird overdue from the river hangs loosely in the foggy night air. The grass sticky with green ink and the

moon's cargo, white light is despatched for the arduous lunar timetable. The few stars out, a football team of survivors mock each other in a drunken orgy

of glow. The chiming of an owl sounds somehow odd in the stillness of night. Then a house, any house, pick one, there, a house on a slant, on an

allotment, once a treed place, is seen in miniature, it draws thoughts from the occasional traveller, the occasional traveller looking out of the plane window

on a crusty cold night and as the plane wing dips, the glint of moonlight reflecting off the suburb below makes those rows and rows of houses and

rows of rows of rows look like record albums resting against a darkened wall, this image can only be imagined with the lantern glare of the moon coming

back in through the plane's bubble glass, a distortion, the streets pressed flat like print on page eight of the government gazette, the houses all buried in the

waves of bitumen, the gentle rollicking colourless waves of suburbia, and as the plane chokes at its gearing ready to land, this suburb is…

Spirit's Hill*

Sit, sit, in hollow tree, on nearby
Spirit's Hill, by the grassy slope.
Hoot, hoot, out of the branches,

whilst the sky thickens dark.
Facial disc of radiated feathers.
Forward facing eyes, acute vision.
Hooked bill – short and sharp.
A bird of prey. Quite violent.

Silent flight and radar-like hearing.
You are the black shirt of the night.
Spectral creature, so forlorn.

A prisoner in broad daylight.
In night's middle not a yawn.
You'll sleep all morn and more.
What a boring arboreal existence.
Daylight, daylight, your head

mechanically from side to side.
No hoot hoot, just quiet please.
Sleep, sleep, in your arboretum.

* Coochiemudlo Island, Queensland

Reading

Past midnight's blank page, fingers of darkness
lonely turn each sheet of silence, words of stars
scurry down deeper into night, while the stump of

time wears away fractionally by ever-present eyes.
Black snow with white footprints, little cut-out
shadows hiding behind their master crystal images.

The last page crinkles over in defiance of time's
weariness, the printed page asleep as the white
glowing cover of morning stirs all into readiness.

Writing Ahead of Myself

Thoughts in unison, and from the heady tribunals of life,
miseries of mind, clandestine and abstract images.
Delving into the mind's pocket, giving me my poetic

blowtorch, dark and omnipresent.
The paper burns with thinking delights, happy paper.
And see a ditch of sand, see what I mean.
Engulfed in a passion of verse, that haunts me to
Heaven and an ice cube placed upon my knee.

Just how long before it goes off onto the floor.
At the laconic beginning I look.
Not glib, radiant nor emblematic.

Tart at times and sure that I'll be back.
Remote is the apple that sits so full of nature.
Leaning forward out of reality I snatch it and
throw and it's bruised and mushed against the wall.
Well I think to myself when things happen

in your mind it's like rubber that wears and tears.
As I write the pocket of my mind dissolves into
a great prism sitting there waiting to be seen.

Night Sky*

Like a hastily drawn map in your mind,
just as sleep beckons.
The edges of which are snug black.
The colour shines like a large belt buckle.
Tear away (as you pulse into sleep) its false skin,
to reveal little stars, a weird new electronic
technique to show you it is dark.

The dutiful moon, the sun's blind stepsister, opens the
door of night and sits awaiting her brother's return.
It is then that the night sky becomes armoured in dreams
as if a plastic-wrapped heart.

Thoughts shuffle into the lift of night, sardine
packed thoughts, little impulses in darkness,
awaiting the coming home of morning.

* Point Danger, Queensland/New South Wales border

I Think of You

Tonight as the sun
is anchored to the
cold west wind and
the moon chugs up

the chimney of night
I think of you, the
fragrance of your body,

the touch of your wet
tongue, the gentle
delight of the soft

strawberriness of the
first kiss of your lips,
elsewhere your silky

wetness covers my flesh
and then I trace the
beads of bones down the

centre of your back,
and then up again to
wetly kiss your neck.

Tonight as the clouds
gather the moon in a
rhythm of dance I close
my eyes and think of you.

Acknowledgements

Thanks to Les Murray, Rosemary Dobson, Judith Rodriguez, Bruce Dawe, Tom Shapcott and Geoff Page for their encouragement and support.

Poems in this collection have appeared in *Australian Writers Journal*, *Brisbane Review*, *Centoria*, *Coppertales*, *Harvester*, *Idiom 23*, *Imago*, *Instead of a Fish*, *Mattoid*, *Micropress Yates*, *New Decade*, *New England Review*, *Public Poetry* (Brisbane Bus Poetry Posters), *Redoubt*, *Rocky Hill Lines*, *Scarp*, *Scope*, *Small Packages*, *Small Times*, *Social Alternatives*, *Spiny Babbler* (Nepal), *Studio*, *Sudden Alchemy*, *The Bulletin*, *The Newcastle Herald*, *The West Australian*, *Verandah*, *Verso* and *Western Word*. A number have been broadcast on Radio 5UV.

'Changing Night' was highly commended in the 1998 Tom Collins Poetry Prize; 'The Ruined Room' was commended in the 1996 Tom Collins Poetry Prize; and 'Bones of Contention' was commended in the 1990 Harold Kesteven Poetry Prize.

The author gratefully acknowledges writer-in-residencies at Ipswich Grammar School (1999), Villanova College (1997), Mabel Park State High School (1997), St Martin's School (1996) and writers' camps at Brisbane Grammar School (1995–97).

Also gratefully acknowledged is the 1997 residency at the Chateau de Lavigny International Writers' Colony, Lavigny, Switzerland, where much of the editing of this manuscript took place.

The author also gratefully acknowledges the 1997 Writer's Fellowship at Charles Sturt University's Booranga Writers' Centre, with special thanks to David Gilbey.

www.ingramcontent.com/pod-product-compliance
Lightning Source LLC
Chambersburg PA
CBHW070313120526
44590CB00017B/2661